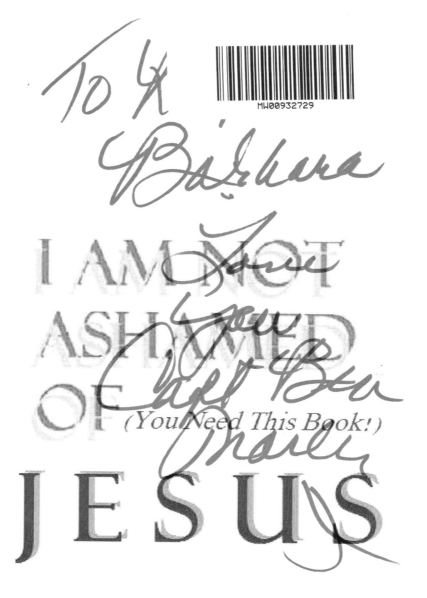

I AM NOT ASHAMED OF

(You Need This Book!)

JESUS

CAPT. BEN MARLER

ISBN:1469903628   ISBN-13: 978-1469903620

DEDICATION

To those in Christ who are meek and fearful and need to be made strong and courageous in witnessing in these last days

IF ANYONE IS ASHAMED OF ME AND MY WORDS, THE SON OF MAN WILL BE ASHAMED OF HIM WHEN HE COMES IN HIS GLORY AND THE GLORY OF THE FATHER AND THE HOLY ANGELS.

LUKE 9:26 ISV

CONTENTS

ACKNOWLEDGMENTS

The messages in this book date from 2009 to the time of publishing in 2012. Scriptural references are from the Amplified (AMP) version of the bible unless otherwise noted. Back cover photo is by Athena Marler Creamer and was taken of her father inside "Capt. Ben's Gifts" at the Emmanuel pier of Capt. Ben Marler's Boat Service, in the mid 1990s. Capt. Ben Marler's Boat Service began in 1934 with Capt. Ben Marler, Sr. on his seine net fishing boat, called the Plymouth, and he carried the first fare-paying customers in Destin, pioneering a party boat industry in the "World's Luckiest Fishing Village." 8 other Marler boats followed: the Stardust, Eureka, Capt. Bennie, Marathon, Her Majesty, Her Highness, Her Majesty II, and last, Emmanuel, which means "God Is With Us." In 2000, Emmanuel was sold to become a whale watching vessel in Virginia Beach, VA, and Capt. Ben retired with his wife to write and enjoy their family in the town where he was born.

CAPT. BEN MARLER

I

WHAT DOES GOD WEAR

Our wonderful Heavenly Father is clothed in faithfulness and crowned with righteousness. Once we can see this our relationship with Him can begin to blossom. Many Christians have a hard time relating to God. Some out right fear Him thinking He hates them or can't wait to unleash His wrath upon them and they are right. Don't get upset with me until I explain this to you. God hates violence and because He does the world was flooded and all air breathing creatures died except for those in the ark with Noah and his family. Can you imagine the scene of those trying to get in after "God" closed the door? It was too late for repentance and they all drowned.

We are approaching a time now when Judgment Day can't be far off. I say this watching Israel and Iran. Iran is preparing to unleash a hell of fire upon Israel and it will bring about a conflagration. All of the countries around Israel will be caught up in it and this is tragic. Our purpose as Christians is to try and reach them with God's love before hand so then have a chance to be saved. We have a terrible enemy, the Islamic religion. This religion founded by the Prophet Mohammed commands his followers to destroy the Jews and infidels, that's you and me.

What they need to understand "by God's grace" that Jesus is God and He died for them like He did for us. His coming to earth and doing the Father's will even to death on a cross is the ultimate righteousness. Few seem to understand the violence brought upon His body. The Passion of the Christ movie was good at revealing the hatefulness of the scourge and it's effect upon a human body. What the Roman soldiers didn't know was each blow that removed flesh creating oozing stripes were for the healing of man's sickness and illnesses. Just as the Blood of Jesus was necessary for us to be washed clean of our sins the stripes are necessary for our healing. I know this is true for I have been healed by them.

The purpose of this message is to allow you to know Him, too, if you don't already. Did you know the worst words in the Bible are those of Jesus when He said to half the virgins in Matthew 25, "I never knew you." These were rejected just as the ones outside the ark as the water rose. If you don't know the Lord please understand He loves you and desires that you repent of your sins so He can give you salvation. See yourself in the ark, for once inside Jesus we are eternally safe.

Our hearts are hard and must be "cracked open" to receive the Gospel message, this is why preaching is necessary. Teaching appeals to the mind but preaching confronts us and deals with our hearts. For instance do you know that every evil thing you've done was placed upon Jesus as He died? Yes, all the things that would make you want to run and hide forever if they were made known. Well, let me tell you they will be made known on Judgment Day if you aren't born again. We who have surrendered our lives to Jesus received an enormous gift, all our sins were erased and forgotten by God. We have been set free from our past forever, Hallelujah!

Anyone who refuses the free gift of eternal life will see their past revealed to all of mankind just before being cast into hell by God's angels. All of this is in the Bible and if you are wise you will make your peace with God right now. Tell Him from your heart exactly how you feel that Jesus was beaten, abused and nailed upon a cross for you personally. If you don't feel anything spend more time meditating upon this fact. God gave us emotions and if the Holy Spirit is there I can guarantee you there will be something happening to you. We need an experience for Satan will come often trying to convince you that you are lost. You can laugh at him and tell him in no uncertain terms, "GO NOW" in Jesus name and he will flee from you.

You have been added to God's eternal family as you received Jesus as your Lord and Master. Now a servant of God you can go before Him and He will anoint you for service. Go today and experience Joy as never before.

2

GOD ISN'T NICE

One of the reasons so few are born again Christians, is they don't understand much about God. The reason is they just can't find the time to read the Bible. They can watch TV until their tails hurt sitting on a couch or chair but just can't turn it off and read what God has to say. When you see how God responds to folks who aren't obedient you will say with me, "God isn't nice." This doesn't mean He isn't Good for He is more than our understanding of the word. He is Holy and His Holiness demands that He not be nice.

Let me explain this for you. God loves us with an unconditional love but not one that allows us to live in disobedience. He sees this as rebellion and since He is preparing a family for eternity and they will be like Him not like the devil. Please read First John 3 and you should see it for yourself. Those who sin "regularly" are not God's kids. He said that, I didn't.   If He was "nice" He would overlook a lot of what we can "little" or small sins. Let me assure you He doesn't overlook any sin and not only that all of them are recorded for Judgment Day. If you are not born again you are walking on the thinnest ice in the world.

Folks are dying constantly. I haven't seen where any funeral homes are going out of business.   Many are making less money due to cremations taking the place of elaborate coffins and accessories. You need to awaken each day and thank God you are alive and make a commitment to do His will "all day long" as you understand it. You aren't working your way into Heaven for Jesus bought that for us by dying on a cross in obedience to His Father. Unless you understand He was dying for you personally [paying for all the sins you have committed or might still commit] you don't have a snowball's chance of becoming born again. When you and I arrive in Heaven that is the common denominator-- we are all born again.

Some have accomplished a lot for the Lord as the Holy Spirit came upon them empowering them to do the "works" God prepared before hand for them. My favorite verse in all the Bible is Ephesians 2:10. Why don't you look it up and see why. I would bet you will use it before long as you want to thank God for sending Jesus to the cross for you. If you don't, please write to me ASAP for you have a big problem. Not only that, but you are depriving yourself of God's Joy. Did you know He said, "I want my joy to be your joy." Consider JOY as pay for obedience!

God isn't nice and it's for our good that He isn't. Once we are all living in Heaven with Him then we will see His "nice side." Right now like a great football coach who is turning boys into men; they aren't nice either. They are demanding of the players to give their best and second best in never acceptable. Are you willing to give you best to God in what ever you do everyday? If you aren't, please tell me why.

When I operated a deep sea fishing business with my wife and mom I never gave less than my best to it. I couldn't have lived with myself for I had dedicated myself to the Lord before I ever reached the pier. I wasn't anywhere as gifted as some of the other captains who also took large groups into the gulf day after day but I was as successful catching fish for my party. I was so dependent upon Jesus He would get the fish ready for me. One day I had a large church group of over 70 aboard and they wanted to have a fish fry at their church when they returned. As I lay in my bed the night before the trip I asked the Lord to help me. He gave me the loran coordinates as to where I was to take them.

Arriving at the spot the water was full of fish and within a few hours the large fish boxes were packed. I was also able to anchor on the place making my day an easy and "great day " in the Lord. I gave Him my best and He gave me His. The fish weren't huge but they caught them two at a time. It was a beautiful thing to see. God is so Good, but not nice. I hope you know Him personally but if you don't please write to me or find me somewhere and I will introduce you to Jesus. He loves you more than I could ever tell you and wants to tell you Himself. Will you allow Him today?

3

WHAT ONLY GOD CAN SEE IN US

You are about to read a most interesting and encouraging word from the Lord so prepare yourself to enjoy it. Not one person has been born by accident. When a man and a woman join their bodies in intimacy [hopefully after holy matrimony] God takes the substances within her and begins to fashion a human being into His likeness. He uses the chromosomes from the mom and dad to give the child some of its features and traits. Then He imprints their identification upon their fingers with prints that are theirs alone. He's never used them before nor will He ever use them again. This alone should make us all feel "special."

Many believe nothing is more valuable than a diamond and they might be right. Let's use the analogy of us being one. Right off the bat at our birth we're admired, and in many cases, treasured by our parents. One thing for sure, we certainly are all treasures in God's sight for He's invested a lot for us. Not only has He taken the time to "knit us together" in our mom's womb but He's made some executive decisions as well. Within us He's placed special gifts, talents and abilities that no one can take away. They are almost like the medulla oblongata or that lower portion of our brain that is programmed to help us breathe without conscious effort along with some other "automatic" functions that help us survive.

Once we're old enough the Holy Spirit sets about liberating us from the curse of sin for it dwells within everyone, or in our lower nature. He begins by allowing us to understand the Gospel message as revealed in the Bible. It says we've all fallen short of the glory of God and unless "modified" can't spend an eternity with Him in Heaven like He desires. So He brings us under conviction by the Holy Spirit who works in our consciousness. We need to recognize the guilt feelings when we do wrong are also a gift, for then will we seek relief from God. He tells us the Truth, Jesus came to save sinners and we're in need of Him. Once we understand God's plan of salvation and submit by receiving Him into our hearts, placing our full trust in Jesus and His work on the cross, God will send His Spirit within us to stay.

But let's not get excited for He's still at work in us. We're still much like a rough and very valuable diamond, but not yet a "gem stone." For example, after a long time of inspection a diamond cutter will locate the flaws before he very carefully breaks a stone. To do this he uses a chisel that's been set in a heavy block of wood and a special mallet. He's marked the exact spot on the diamond using a microscope and where he will perfectly rest the stone. Then with ever so much care he strikes it with his mallet, not too hard or too light.

Then he chooses the best part to begin the process of creating a valuable gemstone. We are like the diamond and should expect God to whack us at some time in the early process. He will not allow any part of this world's effects to remain on us. With great care the gem cutter removes more and more of the stone until one day He says, I'm satisfied. But He's not done for now comes the time of polishing the stone to a luster worthy of His Glory.

Can you see God's plan from the beginning was to have us as His own? Once we've received Jesus the process began and throughout our life God has been at work. This is why the scripture tells us to "rejoice in all things." Some things that happen were extremely hard and we wondered as to way we were going through them, now you know.

After Michelangelo finished his sculpture of David most who've seen have said it's perfect. One man asked him how he was able to do it. His reply is like the one God will use if we ask Him about ourselves. He said, "I simply took everything away from the stone that wasn't David." Once we've received Jesus by faith, God is going to do the same thing, everything about us that isn't Jesus, He's removing. Let's thank Him even before He's finished. If we do, the cutting and whacking may not be so painful.

4

WHAT'S WRONG WITH THE CHURCH

There's an incredible number of folks who claim to be Christians and never go to worship services. I've met some here in Montana on this trip. When I ask where they go they spread their arms and say "right here." They say they commune with God in the out of doors or spaces. This is terrible and only God can do something about it. Perhaps this message can help some to find their way back to fellowship and can help some stay connected.

First of all, please understand true Christianity isn't a religion. There are many man made religions and one God made. The Jews were given a religion through Moses but when I speak with them few follow it. If they do they're called "Ultra Orthodox." I can understand why many remain

Jews when the offer to have an intimate relationship with Jesus is made. They look at us Christians and they don't see Jesus. Allow me to explain, where in the Bible did God say to become divided into denominations? In John 17, a must read, Jesus prays to the Father that His disciples [are you one] might be One even as He and the Father or One. Then He adds, "And not only these but all who will believe in Me through them."

You and I can't bring this about but we sure can pray for God to do it. Actually, He will, for Jesus tells us at the end He is going to send angels to separate the sheep from the goats, the wheat from the tares. He points out the tares will be gathered and burned. I don't know about you, but I don't like that. Jesus paid the same terrible price for those who'll be rejected as He did for those who are chosen. Odds are, the majority of folks who read this message are in danger now. If I had died within the first 33 years of my life I would be facing judgment and condemnation. God would have me cast into hell for I was black in sin. Jesus, even though I believed in Him, had not yet washed me in His Blood. His Blood is the Only thing that can remove sin. If you aren't washed, what are you waiting on?

Religion is hateful and deadly for it attempts to take the place of God's Gift, Jesus Christ. He alone is life. If He isn't in you, He can be. Salvation is from the Lord but He doesn't impose it. Folks, allow me to say, God is picky. Reading the scriptures bears this out for He chose Abraham, Moses, Joshua, Peter, Paul and many others for they would obey Him. He's doing the same today. Did you know, Jesus said, "If you love Me, keep My commandments." Do you think He's kidding? He's deadly serious. If you haven't read Matthew 25 you must do it today. It can help save your life.

Please understand [it seems I have to keep adding this disclaimer] none of our works can save us. Jesus accomplished Salvation while hanging on the Cross. Nothing can be added to His agony and suffering. It was enough! God permitted the sacrifice of Jesus to be all that's needed for anyone to be saved. But, the works revealed in Matthew 25 are incredibly important to God. Read His Words for yourself. You will see He rejects those not doing them. The reason is simple, Jesus isn't in them. That's what the oil and lamps in the chapter are speaking about. The Holy Spirit comes to live in a sinner when he or she is led to the Cross. Until we meet Jesus there how can we truly repent?

WE CAN'T!

God says we must repent [turn around with remorse] of our sins. This doesn't mean, I'm sorry. It means God, I hate my sinful past for Jesus had to die to set me free from it. Do you know that when God forgives us, He has the record of our sins removed from the Books of Judgment? He even removes them from His memory. I'm so thankful for I can also forget them, but never the agony Jesus suffered for me personally.

I've been in God's employment now 39 years [I was born again May 23, 1971.] His Word to me has always been the same. We must be born again. We must "have" Jesus by the Holy Spirit. He wants every Christian to be Baptized by Jesus. Please read and memorize Luke 3:16.

If you're attending a "church" and you aren't praying for the pastor and leadership you're not being a good disciple. Many have been called to the ministry by the Holy Spirit and some just came to it "on their own" and the difference is huge. If your pastor isn't following God's Spirit, go into your prayer closet, pray for him and his family, then ask the Lord if you are to stay in fellowship there. He may not want you there. God has a unique plan for everyone and you may be useful somewhere else. Read Ephesians 2:8-10. Verse 10, God says, "Come and I'll put you to work doing my business."

Please change every prayer into praise, one that exalts the Lord. Jesus said, "If you abide [live] in Me and My Words live in you then ask and it shall be done for you." Read from the scriptures daily. Make God proud of you and you'll be part of His Church and heaven bound.

5

WHAT'S UP WITH CHRISTIANS

Did you know Jesus said, "If you aren't gathering with Me you are scattering?" "If you aren't for Me you are against Me?" I suspect most who claim Jesus as their Savior haven't heard Him say these things. It is a trap to think that once you say, "I believe in Jesus" you are safe. Folks there are many verses in the Bible that tell us there is more to the Christian walk. Do you want to know more? Read on and let's see if we can find out.

In my opinion the most important chapter in the Bible for today is Matthew 25 for the Lord is telling us what He will say to those who loved Him [the least of His brothers] while living on earth and those who didn't. You can argue with me that we are saved by GRACE and I will agree but from that point on there is much to accomplish for Him. In this chapter Jesus pointed out that those welcomed into Heaven are those who fed the hungry, clothed the naked, gave drink to the thirsty, visited the sick and imprisoned and invited in the stranger. Does this sound like "work" to you? Folks it isn't work, it's free flowing love.

Work, in my mind, is what we do to earn something for the effort and time spent. Love is a simple and natural way of living our lives in Him. Do you recall we are told to live in Him and allow His Words to live in us? This means He has absolute control of us in the best sense of the word "control." Jesus isn't a task master but One who leads by His own examples. His disciples watched him in his ministry and then he sent 70 of them to go out and so the same. Do you recall they came back so excited that the devil was subject to them? He told them it was far more important that their names are written down in Heaven. Is your name written down in His Book?

The moment we're born again there's some writing going on in Heaven. Our names are recorded in the Lamb's Book of Life and the Lord is going to keep us in the palm of His hand and no one can snatch us from it either. I can't fathom anyone jumping from it but I suppose we could. This brings up His warnings of the apostasy. Do you know many will fall away in the last days? They will for one reason, they were never born again. Once Jesus is living inside us and we have died to our own life, we are safe. But, for those who attend worship services and live their own lives, too, I suspect they are part of the group that will be lost. I once was one myself.

Why isn't this preached is beyond me. Please read the five chapters of First John and see what the Lord says to you. I call it a book filled with dynamite. It has enough for anyone to come into a saving relationship with God and then, all they will need to walk it out. One of the "gems" within the first chapter is verse 9.

"If we [freely] admit that we have sinned and confess our sins, He is faithful and just (true to His own nature and promises) and will forgive our sins [dismiss our lawlessness] and [continuously] cleanse us from all unrighteousness [everything not in conformity to His will in purpose, thought, and action]. Amplified Bible

I hate to use it, for when I do it means I've strayed from my Lord. Do you recall He gave His life for us so we don't "have to" sin anymore? We sin after temptation once we're born again. Before then it's the natural thing to do for most folks. If we didn't have the 10 Commandments to warn us, most would be breaking them constantly, but not after being born again. If you are one who is sinning all the time I must warn you, you may still be lost. If you are, do what everyone must do, go to Jesus and admit it. As you do, seek His forgiveness and you will find it.

Then do what most don't do, "receive" Jesus as your Lord. I believe we inhale His Spirit when we do. It's His Spirit within us that makes us His. I believe the devil and his angels [demons] believe in Jesus more than any human. They know what's going to happen to them too. Do you remember the demons cast out of the demoniac? After begging Jesus to not be sent to hell and to be sent into some hogs nearby the whole herd of about 2,000 rushed into the lake and drowned.

If Jesus is in you no one has to tell you. I shed a million tears in repentance and was released into freedom to live and love like Him. Before then I was a miserable person even though working hard in my church. Until we are set free by Jesu, we're slaves to our own appetites and desires. This doesn't mean we don't get to do "fun things" afterwards. We do, but they're generally things that bring joy to others, too. Do you want to be one of His? We must surrender to His Lordship for nothing short of it will do!

6

WHAT'S THE BAPTISM IN THE HOLY SPIRIT

It's the power of God that came upon Jesus when He was baptized by John the Baptist at the Jordan. Until this event Jesus was powerless. He'd left His power in Heaven but never forgot who He was and His mission. For about 30 years He lived as a humble and obedient son to Mary and Joseph.

Few seem to understand the Baptism so let's see what John the Baptist is saying in Luke 3:16. "I baptize you with water for repentance but He who follows after me is mightier than me. I'm not worthy to even untie the thongs of His sandals. He Himself will baptize you with the Holy Spirit and with fire."

How much do you think the Lord's disciples could have accomplished, after His Ascension, if the Holy Spirit hadn't fallen on them at Pentecost? Do you remember Jesus met with them 50 days after His Resurrection where He breathed on them so they could be "born again."

Do you remember how excited they were afterwards and when Thomas returned he was doubtful and said, "I won't believe unless I place my finger in the holes of His hands and my hand in His side?" When Jesus returned 8 days later Thomas fell to His knees and said, "My Lord and My God." Isn't it interesting that Jesus didn't correct him?

Is Jesus your Lord and God? If He is, you can be immersed, too. Those who ask are called "Pentecostals" and those who won't are called evangelicals. Both need the power of God to witness effectively. Every disciple is to tell the world about Jesus! Are you verbally witnessing? Some say they witness by their lives but the first disciples went out and shared the Gospel and their testimonies. All born again Christians have a story to tell.

One day God spoke to Joan as she awakened from a nap. "In my Kingdom I have both citizens and soldiers." It excited me, for I now could understand why some denominations are full Gospel and why some aren't. I don't believe this division is His will. Read John 17 to see why.

After my baptism He gave me three very clear dreams. The first revealed the coming collapse of the Roman Church. The second He corrected me as I was advising folks wrongly on reading the scriptures. The third showed me evangelizing criminals in the county jail resulting in a two year jail ministry.

God performed miracles during these visits. I'll never forget some of the most powerful ones. Due to them the sheriff and his wife went into the ministry went he left office! They had witnessed God at work and were led to join a full Gospel church to serve in His power.

I've met some folks who're disappointed after asking God for the anointing and not receiving it. It seems God chooses certain folks for one ministry and others for another based upon what's in their heart. For instance, a man chosen as a pastor has a different attitude than one chosen to be an evangelist. The first is more gentle and caring compared to the second who speaks and acts like a prophet on a mission.

In First Corinthians Paul tell us the gifts of the Holy Spirit are wisdom, knowledge, faith, healing, miracles, tongues, interpretation of tongues, discernment and prophecy. And the Lord gives them as He wishes. I suspect pastors get the best for they care constantly for His sheep. The evangelist needs His power to demonstrate God's love in meeting the needs of those who're lost. It's very hard to resist Jesus' offer when He's just healed you.

The bottom line: God wants us to have His power to witness and so we can grow in our service to Him. Why not ask Jesus to baptize you in His Spirit after you're born again. He said, "Ask and you shall receive."

7

WHEN ALIVE ISN'T LIVING AND DEAD ISN'T DYING

My good friend Greg O'neal asked us to pray for his mom who is in the ICU. I did and continue to uplift her to the Great Physician. This morning while at the gym the Lord spoke again to me about eternal life. His mother is alive but not really living with all the tubes and medical gadgets attached to her. She is "hanging in there" while the Lord uses the finest medical team in her world to keep her going. Greg is a great evangelist who has taken the Good News to many countries where thousands have received the assurance of eternal life. He knows his mom is "safe" but only Jesus knows she's saved. He's lived the life of Jesus before her as well as "preached" it as well. Surely she has made her peace with God who loves her.

How about you? Do you have the assurance that if you were to die today you would spend eternity with the Lord in Heaven? Either you do or you don't. Either way, this message is for you. If you are alive in Jesus you can't die. Jesus said this while standing at the grave of Lazarus. Then He raised him to life while the throng gathered there, gasped. Jesus Christ is God and has made promises that we must hold onto in order to be with Lazarus, and others who placed their full trust in Him. If you tell me you have done that, please don't be offended if I ask you to prove it. If you have you will take delight in my challenge. If you have only partially placed your trust in Jesus, you'll want to argue with me.

How do I know this? Simple, I'm always presenting Jesus to somebody. Those who have Him light up like a bulb. It's as if I clicked a switch inside them and they begin to glow. Why, once they were the walking dead but now they are eternally alive in Him and know it. Salvation isn't us stating some "facts" about Jesus. If you think so, please continue to read and see that our faith in Jesus is just the key to life. Once we say we believe in Him we should remember the devil does too. We must believe that His death on the cross was our death and His resurrection was ours before we can really make the eternal connection by being born again. Salvation is the result of our willingness to die to our will and surrender to Jesus Christ who is Lord. I will not argue with anyone on this for it would be a waste of my time.

Religion has overtaken the Good News and because of it, billions are now enslaved by rules and regulations not directed by the Holy Spirit. If you've submitted to them, I fear for you. You must break free and see Jesus dying for you personally and appeal to Him for His forgiveness.

It's between you and Him. Think of a marriage, isn't it between the man and his wife? Their union isn't between them and their "family tree" of relatives. Having said that, allow me to say, Jesus adds us to the Body of Christ at our being born again of His Spirit. Do you understand that His Holy Spirit comes inside us when we're Saved? It's He who binds us to other born again Christians. His Body is world wide, not in a building or even a denomination. When I was young I was told by a priest in the Catholic Church, if I wasn't a Catholic I'd go to hell. With many tears I told him that I was an Episcopalian and I was going to heaven. He believed his position and I definitely believed mine but we were both wrong.

Jesus didn't go into all the world and make Catholics and Episcopalians, Baptists or any other denomination. No, He said go into to all the world and make disciples. Now let's let some rubber hit the road, are you a disciple? I wasn't until I was almost 33. I could hold my own with anyone who wanted to compare our labors in our church fellowship. There wasn't much I hadn't done or would be willing if asked. The problem, as I learned later, my service was always on my terms, and not God's.

This changed after my wife met Jesus in 1971. Six weeks or so later I met Him in my pastor's office. This "experience" is still with me. That night the Holy Spirit came to my bed where I lay praying. He covered me from my tip toes to my head with His power to witness. I haven't stopped, as you can see reading this message. You can also receive the same power by reading Luke 3:16, understanding what is being said and then asking the Lord to come upon you so you can be a witness, too. If you love Him and are afraid to tell others why, this may be the reason. You have been trying to do it in your power and not His.

Once you're engaged with the Lord nothing is better. You can see He's using you to bring dead folks to life; where their life will never end, even if they should experience a physical death. Sound exciting? You bet and you can start right now. Jesus hangs out at the cross. Go and tell Him how you feel about Him dying for you. Ask Him to forgive you, then ask Him to save your soul. He Will!

8

WHEN DOES JESUS HEAL

I've shared many times the miracle I received after falling from a tree while hunting. My left knee was dislocated and by pulling my body off of it I heard the "pop" as it came back into place. The pain was unbearable and when I cried out to Jesus He sent a man to help me. As we drove along I told him about my cousin who had been hit be a car leaving her near dead. When her husband and sister ran up to her she said, "I'm OK, Jesus is here with me." When I repeated these same words all the pain left instantly, Glory to God! I didn't need an operation or any other treatment. The stripes of Jesus were more than enough. God is faithful and I've experienced it.

This message will bring healing to many once they allow their past understanding of divine healing and grab hold of this TRUTH.

We must understand that Jesus came to save sinners and did so when He died on a cross with every sin ever committed (or would be) was heaped upon Him. Can you imagine the stench that rose to Heaven as He bore them? It's no wonder God the Father deserted Jesus causing Him to cry out, "My God, My God why have you forsaken Me." After this plea the Father must have held His nose and looked back upon His Only Begotten. Please grasp this with all your might for without it how can you and I love Jesus enough?

The truth is we can't and this is why we see "Christians" having to be recommitted, some over and over. Personally, I don't believe these folks are born again [yet]. We who enjoy intimacy with Jesus have it as a duty and a privilege to not judge those outside His family but always be reaching out to them. The LOVE of God inside us is all we need so let it loose and see Him redeem them for Himself.

If you think about it Jesus actually accomplished three

things as He died. One He shed His Blood so the Father could wash us clean as we repent and accept Jesus as our Lord. He is also our Savior but that will be realized on Judgment Day. Please don't go around calling Jesus your Savior if you aren't walking in obedience. Didn't Jesus say, "Why do you call me Lord, Lord and not do what I say?" Yes He did and few seem to hear it.

As He hung in agony the pain from the beating ministered by the brute Roman Soldiers with a scourge that lacerated His body, leaving stripes which were bloody welts. Bits and pieces of His flesh had been removed with each blow. This is a historical fact and the moment we look upon them trusting His agony and sacrifice for us, healing will flow to us. Don't struggle with this just do it. When I feel "ugly" I instantly go to the Lord and thank Him for being beaten nearly to death FOR ME! If you are born again please consider healing as part of your inheritance for it is.

Jesus defeated Satan at the Cross and everything that He accomplished is ours as we receive Him into our hearts as LORD. Please memorize John 1:12 for it is paramount to our relationship. "To as many as those who receive Him [Jesus] gave He the power to become the children of God, even those who believe in His Name." I will never forget the day the Holy Spirit illuminated this verse to me. For at least 30 days it was the only thing I wanted to speak about. At Last, the Lord allowed me to understand that Salvation isn't an intellectual exercise but an experiential one. Just as you are breathing now and living, once we inhale Jesus by faith we live forever.

Billions believe that simply believing in Jesus will get them saved. Doesn't Satan and his huge hoard of hateful demon spirits believe in Jesus and tremble? You are right they tremble for they know where they are going when God is through using them. I believe all illness, disease and sicknesses come from Satan. Read the Book of Job and you can see how this works. God only allows Satan so much room to work, and then only to bring humans to a place where they will come to Christ. Many are suffering and never come, which is our fault. We have tons of God's love inside us but it has been dammed up.

The Lord has told us that from our bellies would flow LIVING WATER. It can happen when we release it but will not burst out like a volcano until then. Do you want to see folks saved? Love them, lift them up to the Lord boldly and pray for God to reveal Himself in Jesus. In 1st John we are told, "Those who have Jesus have eternal life and those who have not Jesus have not eternal life." Do you believe Him? If you do then release Jesus inside you to those headed to judgment and death. If you don't may I suggest you come up with a very good excuse that God will accept; you will need it.

I would rather pray for a sick person than anyone, for I know Jesus, and He is more than willing to meet their need. I often have while reading in the Bible where He healed the sick, delivered the possessed, raised the dead and forgave those who repented. Remember the criminal dying next to him who repented? Jesus forgave Him instantly and told him that He was taking him to Paradise. Sadly, the other criminal refused to repent and was lost. We must work while there is still light. That light is Jesus inside you!

9

WHEN WILL JESUS RETURN

One thing's for sure, lots of folks don't think it will be any time soon. Have you noticed how few make it to worship services? I used to say to people, tomorrow is Sunday, where would you like to be if Jesus returned then? Without exception they would say "In Church." This revealed several things, they didn't know what the Bible teaches. Like, those who are "born again" are the Church. We've become part of the "world wide" Body of Christ. We are like tiny bits of Jesus and one day we'll be welcomed in Heaven. Those not "in Him" will not be allowed. His offer of forgiveness and inclusion into His eternal family is still available. If you haven't been included, God says, "Today is the day of salvation." Make it yours, OK?

Jesus told His disciples that only the Father knows when the end times will come. Lets remember, we who "have" Jesus will one day simply disappear in a flash. You need to read First Thessalonians 4:13-18 carefully and slowly so the Lord can impress upon you His Words. There are some who think that this upward call to glory will happen before the horrible tribulation, some during it and some after it occurs but all believe it will happen and it's clear who will be included. First, the dead "in Christ" and then we who are alive [in Christ] will be taken up. Notice it doesn't say those who believe in Him. One thing for sure you don't want to be here when the tribulation time arrives.

Becoming born again is the only way we can enter into God's promise of eternal life. No amount of religion, works or supposed "goodness" can accomplish it. Becoming born again is so important that Jesus said we MUST BE to even see the Kingdom of God. Born again means the Spirit of God is alive in us and leading us to do the works that God prepared beforehand. It's a shame that billions don't understand this and yet say, "I'm a Christian." They've been led to believe that since they are a member of a denomination and/or have made a proclamation it was enough to be saved.

I did all that myself and was still as lost as a goose in a snow storm. Until I came to understand that Jesus was hanging on the cross for me personally there wasn't any way I was willing to surrender my life to Him. When I did I died to my will [I'm still at it,] and asked God to forgive me for my numerous sins. The effect of His forgiveness still lingers as I melted before the Lord. When I asked Jesus to come into my heart it was the most wonderful day in my life.

I literally experienced forgiveness where tons of guilt left in a single second. Never had I ever felt so wonderful. That night the Holy Spirit came to my bed and anointed me. I felt a "ripple like" motion began at my toes, it rushed up to my lips and a language called the "language of angels" began to flow. I knew it was a flow of praise for God's goodness to me. For the last 39 years this gift has allowed me to communicate with my Heavenly Father on a level my mind isn't capable.

All born again Christians should seek this Baptism in the Holy Spirit. It's promised in Luke 3:16 and you can see its effect in the Book of Acts. The Baptism is given to help us witness. "When the Holy Spirit comes "upon," you shall be my witnesses, etc." Witnessing isn't difficult if we've experienced "something." It's like seeing two automobiles collide at an intersection and giving the police a witness report. If you didn't see what happened, only heard a noise, your testimony wouldn't be of much use. Nothing is more important for a Christian than to be in a wreck. When you and the Lord collide, I guarantee the results will be positive. You will discover He has such a great plan for your life. There isn't any way you would believe it even if He were to tell you.

I discovered how to access His plan after He led me to use Ephesians 2:10 as the basis for a daily commitment and I've used it for somewhere about 35 years now. My life has been full of joy as I've seen and experienced the Lord do things that I still rejoice over. For instance, a woman was crying at the altar rail. When I asked why, then she told me she had a bad heart and was going back to Atlanta for an operation and was so afraid. I told her, Jesus can heal hearts, would she like me to pray for her. She uttered a tearful "yes." Then I simply said, "Lord Jesus, thank you for healing her heart."

About a month later she and her husband returned to Destin. After the worship service she came up to me and said, "The doctors were so excited, they couldn't find a thing wrong with my heart." I can't tell you how much joy this brought me. Jesus is also our Healer, Amen? I believe He's coming back soon, do you? If you do, prepare by becoming born again right away.

10

WHO SAID YOU CAN'T GO TO HEAVEN

One thing for sure, it wasn't Almighty God. Did you know Jesus came to save sinners? We've all sinned and fallen short of His Glory but that can change in a few minutes. God requires us to become born again and it's not complicated at all. He said He made the Gospel [Good News] simple to confound the wise. Now if you're wise, this may be more difficult for you but definitely not impossible.

Jesus died on a cross at the command of His Father, Almighty God. Why, for He loves everyone and wants all of us to repent [turn away from sinning] and to receive Jesus into our hearts so He can adopt us into His family. God allowed Roman soldiers to whip Jesus with a terrible whip called a scourge that nearly killed Him before He died upon the cross. The wounds from the beating give us a place to look when we need healing in our bodies. He said, "By His stripes are you healed." When Jesus died, every sin, sickness and disease was upon His body. All God requires is we believe it.

Salvation faith isn't common or ordinary, instead it requires much more from us. God wants us to die to our will first and this is really difficult for some. Jesus is Lord which means the One who is God Emmanuel [or with us]. He isn't someone whom we can argue with but the One whom we obey as we live daily in His care. To make it possible, He's given to us His Own Holy Spirit inside us. As we live in Him the things we read of Jesus doing in the Bible, we will do. I've seen the mighty works of God and in some cases been involved in them.

Will you surrender to Jesus today? There isn't a single "good" reason not to for you were born to live eternally with Him. He tells us only a few will be saved. The fact you've read this far is proof to me you are one who can become a child of God. Please turn from all religion for it's not of Him. Relationship is of Him and He wants you to have it so you can become a trusted and valuable servant for Him. Don't turn Him down for if you do He can't save you.

The decision is always ours. He made His decision for you the same day you were conceived in your mom.

Right then He said, "I love you and I'm giving you gifts, talents and abilities which no one can take away from you. To prove they are from Me, I'm giving you finger prints that are yours alone."

"Don't doubt me for a second, look around and see my handiwork. I created it all for you to enjoy. Look up and see the Heavens above for this is where your future lies. The earth upon which you stand will be removed by a terrible fire. Everything on it will be destroyed, not one thing will survive. In its place I'm going to recreate it in perfection. Then I'm going to lower down the great city, The New Jerusalem. You and I will live in it with all those who love Me. My city is 1500 miles cubed with streets of pure gold."

"Your new body is already prepared for you and it is perfect and beautiful too. You will never hunger, thirst or suffer pain with Me. I will be all you need forever. Today is the day of salvation, please don't refuse my offer. I paid a huge price for you by allowing my Son Jesus to die in your place. Understand His death was important, for then I could raise Him back to life. His resurrection will be yours as you receive Him into your life. Many millions have before you and millions will afterwards. I want you to be My child today."

11

WHY ARE YOU AFRAID?

Jesus was amazed when his disciples awakened Him from sleep as their small boat began to fill up with water. They were experienced fishermen and knew before long they were going to have the boat sink from under them. As a modern day boat captain even with all the modern life saving equipment aboard our vessels, sinking isn't something I would look forward to experiencing. For one, they had no life jackets and maybe weren't that strong of swimmers especially in the stormy waters they were battling. I can see them bailing water as fast as they can but not gaining at all.

Jesus seemed surprised that they were so afraid for He had been with them for some time now and they already knew He was someone very special. But why didn't He wake up and realize the grave danger facing them? The answer might surprise you, Jesus is Almighty God in the flesh. Yes He is Emmanuel, God with us. Mary was told by the angel Gabriel that her son would be called Emmanuel or God with us. She was the only one who knew for sure when she delivered Jesus that she was still a virgin. Joseph had been told she was, and to his credit, he treated her as one, even when she turned up pregnant. We who are born again know by experience that Jesus is God for He lives in us. This is what born again means.

When Jesus spoke to the wind it stopped immediately and the sea became calm leaving his crew of disciples stunned. "Who is this that can calm the wind and waves with a word" was their open statement to each other. I can see some standing there looking like deer in the headlights for they still didn't know. This is true today for many Christians. They go to worship services and duly place money in the offerings, not really knowing that Jesus is God. I've heard many call Him, "The man upstairs" or some other name that reveals they don't have a clue. If you know Jesus is God, I hope you are not offending Him by living a life of fear.

Fear is a spirit and not one you and I should welcome but resist in the Name of Jesus and watch it go. This message is to help you gain the confidence to use the Name of Jesus as the evil spirits are about to make inroads in the church. We are already into a severe downturn in the economy and with the polices being followed by the current administration it will continue to go down. Now this doesn't mean it will effect us in a negative way for God has made some awesome promises to His children. Please read John 1:12 to see who His kids happen to be. This is a necessity for all of us so do it!

One of the things my wife and I learned about 30 years ago is that it is more blessed to give than to receive. When we lined up with the Word of God our life was far more enjoyable. This doesn't mean we didn't work for we did and the 14-15 hour days took a toll on us but we were young "back then" and could do it. God didn't tell us to give everything away but to make it available to the Holy Spirit. Looking back I have some memories that are absolutely priceless [no pun intended] when the gift was really not that much money. I just followed my heart and God did the rest.

Many are fearful now of being able to make their mortgages and to pay their other debts and it may look impossible but Jesus said, "Nothing is impossible with God." Our job is to believe Him. In Hebrews 11:6 we learn that, "Without faith it is impossible to please God for we must believe that He is and He is a rewarder of them that diligently seek Him." Pay close attention to the word diligently. This means to spend time with Jesus asking the Holy Spirit to help you.

As you seek the Lord, know in your heart that He is on your side, because He is alive in you. This alone should relieve you of fear. You are not a mortal now, you are an immortal and can not die. Oh, your body might stop working, as everyone's does, but the real you is instantly alive forevermore with Jesus. "To be absent from the body is to be with the Lord." "Precious in the sight of the Lord is the death of His saints [true believers]."

I suspect most of us have more anxiety over the safety of our family than any other thing. Well if so, let's commit them to the Lord each day and trust Him to guard them with His angels. Danger lurks everywhere but so does our

Omnipresent God.

Coming to understand who you are in Christ is the real secret of living in the gift of God's Peace or Shalom. It is ours as we accept it. Like someone offering you a gift, it isn't yours until you take it into your possession. Will you take Jesus now as your Lord? He isn't anyone's Savior until He is the Lord of their life; trust me in this. I know from my own experience it is true, and so do millions more. If you need more please ask. I have many messages that can help you.

12

WHY DOES GOD LOVE US

You may be the meanest person you know and have done things that you are so ashamed of, but trust me in this, God never stopped loving you. He is Agape or unconditional love. He created you from the "ingredients" supplied from your mom and dad. When they united, He began to knit you together in her womb and the first thing He told you was, I LOVE YOU! He didn't whisper it either. With great joy He embraced you in His love and gave you everything you needed to survive outside the womb. While in there He watched over you as you began to come to the image of God Himself.

Even if your parents wanted you with all their hearts and even prayed long and hard for you to arrive, you were always God's idea. Hold on to this truth so the world can

not steal you from Him. As you know by now, Satan runs
this world and we are like pawns between him and God, the
Lord. Satan will use every trick in the book to deceive you.
He is a liar, thief, murderer and accuser who wants you
dead. He has been very successful, and the vast majority of
people born have died and are facing judgment. I can make
you a promise you won't be with them if you care to believe
Jesus came to die for you. When you fall in love with Him
and receive Him into your heart [life] you have become an
immortal. His Life in you is eternal and now you are too.

There is a cost that I've discovered. First, and most
important, we must give up this life to have His. No one can
live two lives with God. Many try and fail, for Jesus can't be
your Lord until He is inside you. You can try and follow Him
but you will fail over and over, until you must give up. Jesus
doesn't come to us to argue. He is Emmanuel, or GOD WITH
US. Until we understand this, we will be subject to every
religious spirit that comes our way. In Romans 8 God tells
us, "The sons of God are those who follow the Spirit of
God." From experience, permit me to tell you, until He is the
Lord of your life you can't follow Him.

The Word of God tells us that God doesn't share His Glory with anyone. He is Almighty God and millions and millions of angels are at the Throne worshipping Him all the time. He isn't someone to ignore or dismiss as "The man upstairs." He has also told us that He won't strive with man forever. He has a plan for everything and this includes our life, but He will not force us to love Him which really means "obey Him."

Hopefully with this settled, allow me to tell you something that most Christians don't know. God has a divine plan for your life, and it is beyond your wildest imagination in scope. God loves us so much, He allows us to do the things He can do, by simply speaking them. He wants us to be just like Jesus, as strange as that may sound. If that is in your heart too, then there is a time coming when He will say to you, "Well done my good and faithful servant, enter now into the joy of your Master." Matthew 25

His love grows and grows for us as we walk in obedience with Him. Do you recall how He said, "David is a man after my own heart for he wants to do my will"? You may recall God had David anointed by the prophet Samuel so that God's power would rest upon him. When Goliath stood there cursing David he was also cursing the Lord. When the stone left the sling it went right between his eyes knocking him to the ground. God didn't need David to knock him down but he was lifting David up before the whole army of Israel. When David took Goliath's sword and took off his head it was for our benefit. The devil is God's enemy and with the sword of the Holy Spirit [the scriptures] we can also take down Satan.

God loves us so much we have a written record of His will in the Bible. In America we have millions that have never been opened. Until we open ours and begin to feast upon it we can not inwardly digest it. Once inside us the mighty things of God are not only possible but a sure thing. I have some testimonies to back this up. Will you allow God to use you? If you will then go to the Bible for instructions. As you do the Love of God will come over and within you to flow out like a river of life to a world that needs a refreshing drink of Jesus. Will you do it? If you won't, prepare to give God a very good reason why you didn't.

He will still love you but I'm not sure he will be real happy. Let's live daily to make Him smile at us. OK?

13

WHY ME LORD

I suspect nearly everyone has reached the place where they uttered these words. Most of the time it was when something bad has happened to them. This message isn't about the negative but is very positive, Jesus loves you.

You and I know so many things we've done for which we're so ashamed. I did many but Jesus said we aren't to look back on them for if we do, we aren't worthy of the Kingdom of God. I don't know about you but I'm so relieved to hear them. Why would the Lord say such a thing?

Let's understand that the Bible is written for everyone but

only applies to those who will submit their lives to Jesus. What good is it to pray the "Lord's Prayer" when you don't mean it? For instance how can God be your Heavenly Father if He hasn't adopted you? The Truth is He can't. This message will help you come to the place that He will, but let me warn you it is going to cause a major change in your life style. A friend of mine became very angry with our pastor after his wife found an intimate relationship with Jesus. She didn't want to go out and party anymore like before. Her relationship with Jesus was almost too much for him.

God allowed me to be one of many who witnessed to him and got through his great intellect. Once he came to Christ as his Lord, great things have happened to him. I'll be so bold as to say he would have died over 30 years ago had he not become a born again Christian. Trust me in this for I feel cautioned by the Lord to not share more about him. He is one of my favorite people on the planet. I love him with all my heart for his life impacted mine. By the way, he was asking God, "Why me?"

Please understand we weren't born to die and be buried in

a box in a cemetery. If you and I are born again Christians, before the funeral or memorial service begins we're already with our Savior. "To be absent from the body is to be with the Lord;" "Precious in the sight of the Lord is the death of His saints" are two of my favorite Bible verses. Jesus told the criminal who repented next to Him while dying on his cross, "Today, you shall be with Me in Paradise." Isn't it interesting that Jesus didn't say, "When you die they will bury you and one day I'll come and get you." After seeing my dad in his resurrected body in a dream four years after Jesus took him I know this scripture is true.

If you are suffering now from a terrible disease and you are a born again Christian what are you doing about it? You probably have been to a doctor and been given some medicine or have received some treatment like radiation but is that all you're going to do? Chances are that it is, for no one has preached that Jesus is willing to heal you. Everyone knows He is able but few realize He is the same yesterday, today and forever as the scriptures teach us. I know God is still in the healing business for I've experienced it and have been blessed to extend his hand to some suffering.

During the thirty plus years I've been writing what He places in my heart, I've shared many testimonies but I will share this one again to show you just how willing the Lord is to heal. I was ministering communion at the altar rail of our church here in Destin when I came upon a woman crying. I knelt down close to her and whispered, why are you crying? She looked up and said, "I have a bad heart and when I get back to Atlanta the doctors are going to operate on me and I'm so afraid." I said, I believe Jesus can heal hearts do you believe it too? She gave me a sobbing yes and then I placed my hand on her and simply said, "Thank you Jesus for healing her heart."

About a month later she and her husband returned to Destin and again at the altar she asked me if I remembered her. I said no for I was taking hundreds fishing every week. Then she said, "You prayed." I instantly pointed to the exact place at the altar where we first met. Then she said, "When I returned to Atlanta the doctors couldn't find a thing wrong with my heart." Glory!

Jesus honored our faith and like the woman who touched his garment power poured from our Lord to her. He is still doing this all over the world as I write this for you. So, before you go to the Lord with a "Why me Lord" why not give your life totally to Him and become born again of His Spirit.

By the faith He's given you, accept the benefits of the horrible suffering He endured. His stripes provide healing and His Blood washes us as clean as new snow. His victory over Satan is ours, too. We are told, "Greater is He that is in you than he [the devil] who's in the world." Do you believe it? If you do, go to Jesus the Great Physician first. He is our healer!

14

WHY WORSHIP JESUS

Folks, I hope this message will bring you to your knees. Jesus is God Almighty in the flesh. There is a day coming when everyone will fall on their knees and proclaim Him to be Lord, even if He wasn't their Lord.

At this time we need to be on our knees daily worshipping Him, for He not only created us but came and died a horrible death so the Father could forgive us of our countless sins. What do you think will happen if we don't? Do you think the Lord is going to brush off our lack of respect and adoration of His Only Begotten?

If you do, please change your mind right now, for eternity could be seconds away. Not one of us knows the exact second we will die and as I write, millions are close to leaving this world for the next. Some are seconds from an automobile wreck that will kill them. Others are near a massive thrombosis like the one that took my dad in 1970. I was with him a few hours earlier and he seemed fine to me. He wanted me to have lunch with him and some others but I'd planned to go to Panama City with a friend who was going to hunt in Alaska with me. A fellow with a lot of experience was going to give us some tips. I wish I had known God was going to take Him.

When I was ushered into the emergency room where my dad's still body lay, I was absolutely devastated and wept uncontrollably. Then standing next to him I recall praying, "Lord, thank you that this man was my daddy." If anyone in the world was ready to meet Jesus that day it was him. I've written a lot about my dad's devotion and labors for Jesus but the majority I never knew. Afterwards folks would tell me of ways he had blessed them. One, a young man on his way to seminary with a wife and children and no money, found in the note that my dad handed them contained a lot of it. We never knew he did this until several years later. The fellow ended up being elected the Bishop of Texas in the Episcopal Church.

My dad was in love with Jesus, and I would like to know some day that my love for Him is as close. You might say, I'm working on it. You can too if you come to know Jesus. Knowing about Jesus is not knowing Jesus. Just as I feel many are still lacking intimacy and true knowledge, I too was a stranger. Jesus wants to come and live inside everyone but can't if we refuse to repent. Please understand repentance isn't simply saying I'm sorry. It means we recognize that our sins are hateful in the sight of God and must be washed in His Blood.

Can you see your sins on Him? If you can't, go to a quiet place where you can sit with Him. God wants us to fall in love with Jesus not simply say, "I love Jesus." If anyone should ask we should be able to say, Jesus is my Lord and God. He has led me to freedom to do and be all He intended when He created me. Or, I'm in the process of being led.

Jesus isn't who most think. He isn't the "man upstairs" or some other unflattering label. He is the One who holds the whole universe together. Please read the first chapter of Colossians for an eye opening. Every atom is bound together by His might. He created everything you see and all that you don't see. We have submarines that can reach incredible depths and return with photos of creatures never seen before by man. Our electron microscopes reveal life forms that was only suspected before. The Hubble telescope is still opening the heavens as never before. What we can see is breathtaking. Do you understand why we should worship Him all the time?

Worship is a privilege and not a right. For us who have become born again, it's like breathing. All our thoughts and actions will hopefully bring glory to Jesus. We know He always knows what we are thinking for His Holy Spirit is within us. In Romans 8 we are told, "The sons of God are those who follow the Spirit of God." May I humbly ask, are you doing them? If not, would you consider using the verse He gave me over 30 years ago and get busy? "For we are His workmanship created in Christ Jesus unto good works that God Himself prepared for us to walk in." Ephesians 2:10

I've changed it from plural to first person singular, "Good morning Father, Good morning Jesus, Good morning Holy Spirit, I'm your workmanship, etc." Then I commit to do whatever He has for me. Any born again Christian can do the same. If you aren't born again you should become one today, time is wasting. If you need my help please ask for I may also be seconds away from going home now. I'll be 72 in July and that's a long ways past my dad's 59. He's waiting on me with my mom, God showed me this and I want to see Jesus face to face. Do you want to see Him?

15

A FIRESTORM IS APPROACHING AMERICA

What you are about to read isn't something I will enjoy writing, but how can I not place here what the Holy Spirit is saying to me. Have you watched the fires that rage ruthlessly in the west on TV? They consume all before them and after passing, there isn't anything left but devastation. You and I can prepare for what's coming by spending time on our knees before the Lord. God hears and answers prayer, He's promised to do it. He says, "If two or three will gather together [in spirit] and agree as on touching anything I will do it." Why would He make such a statement? Why because He lives inside the born again Christians [his kids] and the prayers will be from the Holy Spirit.

Do you know the Holy Spirit? In Acts some who had been baptized with John's baptism [of repentance] didn't even know there was another baptism. In Luke 3:16 we're told that Jesus is the One who baptizes in the Holy Spirit and with fire. Fire fights fire, folks, and those who place their lives in danger fighting forest fires use this technique a lot. They back fire or consume areas before the raging flames arrive. This creates "barriers" which can slow or end the fire. Many times though the embers can "jump" the space already burned and restart the fire again.

If you're concerned about your family and loved ones, isn't it time for you to go to Jesus and ask Him to baptize you in the Holy Spirit? When He does you'll receive His power to witness. At last you'll have the ability to approach anyone, even those who are hostile, to tell them that Jesus loves them. When you do, you can back it up with your own story of Amazing Grace.

Please understand, all that is happening to America now is because of sin. God is Almighty God, and He's going to bring Judgment to those who are hostile towards Him and His Son, Jesus. Few preachers are telling the lost to repent or they'll be caught up in eternal fire. Do you hear it where you worship? Do you see folks responding to the warning?

Part of the responsibility of a child of God is to pray for the teachers and preachers whom the Lord has raised to equip the saints for service. There are five ministries mentioned, apostles, prophets, evangelists, pastors and teachers. Only in some instances do you hear of the apostle and prophet anymore. Their ministry is just as important now as ever. So pray that the Lord will bring whomever He has chosen to fore so the Gospel can be preached and obeyed all over the world. Don't be one who believes the Lord is content with us living lukewarm lives. He's told us He will spit us out of His mouth if we are.

Are you willing to tell God often how much you love Him and then prove it by submitting to the Holy Spirit? If you aren't, what do you expect Jesus to say to you on Judgment Day? How can He say, "Well done my good and faithful servant, enter now into the joy of your Master." He can't and He won't, for He always keeps His Word. Please stop now if you have your Bible near and read Matthew 25. Jesus is saying these things and we had better listen.

We can't be saved by our works, for we are saved by faith and that's not of ourselves but from a faith given to us by God as a gift. But is your faith real? In James we are told, I will show you my faith [genuineness] by my works. Are these things [works] something we've decided to do on our own? Of course not, they're works prepared beforehand by God our Father for us to do. Read it for yourself in Ephesians 2:8-10. Accept these Words and live with God forever. Remember, everything on earth will be burned up one day. His Word written in our hearts is eternal. This is why we should read and digest the Word and allow it to strengthen us so we can serve Him.

The vast majority of folks who say they're going to Heaven have no Biblical discipline. Their major complaint, "I don't have time" but don't they have time to watch TV? Make sure the Lord doesn't say the worst words in the Bible to you, "I never knew you." We must be born again to know Him.

Please believe me there is safety only when we are in Jesus. Do you remember the fiery furnace into which the Persian King had three of God's servants thrown? And when he looked, he saw there were now four. Jesus was in there with them protecting and keeping them safe. When they were removed them wasn't even the smell of smoke on them. This Jesus is the same yesterday, today and forever. Folks, we can count on Him. Can He count on us?

16

CHRISTIANITY ISN'T A POPULARITY CONTEST

We'd really be weird if we didn't want folks to like us. Many try hard to make friends and are very successful. Some who try, can't even get a puppy to like them. After 39 years of serving the Lord, as good as I can, I've failed miserably in creating a large group of "friends." Jesus warned us if we followed Him we would be persecuted. Reading the Bible we see this is true. Paul had some very close friends but far more enemies. Reading his letters to the Churches clearly bears this out. I suspect when we arrive in Heaven we will see he was greatly rewarded. How about you, do you have lots of friends? I hope you do, and all are working for Jesus.

Do you remember the story of the Prodigal? When he left home with a sizable fortune [half his dad's wealth] he went to a foreign country where he had loads of friends until his money ran out. I suspect many are like that today. They're desperate for love and when in a bar or restaurant buy everyone a round of drinks. For a few moments the claps on the back and the cheers that embrace him makes it seem the expenditure was worth it, but trust me, it was a waste. We have only One true friend and that's Jesus.

Please don't think I'm saying we can't have friends, for we all do. I have a tiny number that I can count on for anything at anytime. They truly love me and I love them, too. They have shown me their affection by being there for me when I was truly hurting. They didn't have compassion, but empathy, which means they actually hurt with me. I hope in your group there are some like these treasured souls.

Jesus is always with me for He's in me. If you aren't born again, He isn't in you. Religion has taken the place of intimacy; I know for I was very religious until I melted before Him. Lets get the rubber on the road, have you experienced the New Birth? The Bible tells us we become a New Creation when we die to our old life and are filled with His. Has that happened to you? You aren't answering to me but to the One who is having me write this message.

God loves everyone, actually He's in love with us. He proved it by sending Jesus to the Cross to die. Had Jesus not shed His Blood on the cross not one person could be saved, not the Pope, Billy Graham, or even St. Paul. Please understand, our sins have condemned us to hell. Only the Blood of Jesus can wash us clean. God does this "after" we surrender our lives to Christ.

The vast majority of folks calling themselves Christians haven't experienced salvation. If you don't believe me, ask "Christians" you meet to share their testimony. When I do it I hear over and over, "My religion is personal." Well I'm sure it is, but can it be the relationship with Jesus offered by God? I have to question it, for part of the "deal" is we are to share our testimonies as led by the Holy Spirit. If this wasn't true, why are you still here after being born again? The instant Jesus cleansed you with His Blood and entered your heart, you're a citizen of Heaven. All those who refuse Jesus will be turned away. I don't enjoy writing this, but it's the TRUTH. Can you see why some folks don't like me? They didn't like Jesus either and He's the TRUTH. He's also the "only" WAY and the LIFE. If He isn't in you, consider yourself lost.

In Romans 6, you can read what Baptism is all about. The water is a grave and we are to be buried in it [hard to do if sprinkled]. When uplifted, we breath air [Spirit] which can sustain life. The Holy Spirit is Eternal Life. Oxygen in our air supplies the main ingredient for physical life. Air without oxygen will cause death in short order. Christianity without the Holy Spirit will also kill you. "The wages of sin is death" and until we "receive Jesus" we're dead in God's sight even when walking about. It's like dead men and women walking and most don't know it. This message can fix that.

God says, "Friendship with the world is enmity with Him." If you're in love with your possessions, are in pursuit of more, I hope you'll go on your knees to God admitting it. Wealth isn't sinful, as a matter of fact, we need extra wealth to help those whom the Lord shows us who are in need for we can't give away what we don't have. The Government does, for we are being heavily taxed so the "rulers" in Congress can buy votes.

Jesus isn't into buying your vote but winning your heart. He's always there for you 24 / 7 and will be there to claim you on Judgment Day. You and I can get to make the choice. Will you become born again? If you haven't, do it now. Do you need help? Please ask.

17

BROTHERS AND SISTERS WE ARE OUTNUMBERED

I love Sarah Palin for the same reasons that those on the left hate her. She's my sister in Jesus and they can't stand to see a true born again Christian prosper in anything. Jesus promised us persecution and folks, she's getting it by the boat load. What they don't know is they are adding to her reward with God. How important it is for us to serve the Lord openly too so we too can hear Him say, "Well done My good and faithful servant, enter now into the Joy of your Master." Do you think He will say that to you? If not, this message can be of great value to you.

There aren't many Christians who can give a testimony that is exciting and attractive. I'm not saying they all have to be that way for some folks are going to come to the Lord like a tree growing in the yard. The problem is most of them never do anything but show up for services and do as little as possible in sharing Christ with the world. But those who have experienced the fantastic joy of being set free from a life of sin in a single day are so excited they want to tell everyone. I know this is the case for me. I was as miserable as one could be, until May 23rd in 1971 when I receive a full pardon from God and adoption into His family. While sitting on a chair in my pastor's office, God redeemed me and made me one of His kids.

Sometimes I think the Lord allowed me hit the bottom so He could uplift me. My wife had met Jesus in our living room about 6 weeks before and came running to the bed where I was asleep so excited I thought there was an intruder in the house. I was reaching for my gun when she told me what had just happened to her. While on her knees telling God that she loved Him, Jesus came into the room. She said the whole room lit up. I know one thing for sure, she did. For a very long time she walked around reading the Bible or a book on the Holy Spirit in her hands. I'm so blessed to have her as my wife of almost 52 years now for the Jesus inside her has brought me to know Him, too.

Be honest now, do you know Jesus or do you know about Him? Don't feel bad if you can only say you know about Him for that was my condition. I had to surrender my life, all of it, to know Him. My life since that wonderful day has been filled with excitement and sometimes persecution, too. Jesus said, "If you aren't for Me you are against Me. If you aren't gathering you are scattering." Doing what He wants will always bring fire from the enemy, and our sister in Christ, Sarah Palin, is under a barrage of hateful artillery. I hope you will adopt her and her family in your prayers today. She was born, like you and me, to love and serve the Lord. She's an excellent example of how God works to accomplish His will here on earth. I've read her book Going Rogue and now my wife is reading it. Hopefully everyone will, for in it you will see someone who loves America and our Constitution. She loves people and they love her, too. I trust you've seen the crowds who show up when she does.

There's a day coming when we all will stand before the Lord for reward if we are born again. No amount of religion can save us. We must be "in Jesus" for it's His righteousness, gained by obedience, that makes us acceptable to the Father. We who've been buried with Him in Baptism and raised with Him in His Resurrection are already living in our eternal life. No one can kill us, for we are now immortal as He is immortal. Realizing this allows us to serve Jesus in spite of persecution.

I suggest we watch Sarah as we pray for her. God is going to protect her and keep her for Himself just as He will for you and me. Isn't He wonderful? You bet He is, and one day we will see Jesus face to face.

Right now we are to commit our lives daily to His service. I've used Ephesians 2:10 for over 30 years doing it. Please do the same and allow God to use you in adding to His family. This isn't hard to do at all. Please take the time to write out your salvation story. It doesn't have to be long or fancy, just truthful. I wish folks had a long and short version ready for when given the privilege to share our love of Jesus we can do one or the other. I use my "one minute" testimony all the time.

Folks want to know why you are different so tell them. We

have the peace of the Lord, "There is therefore no condemnation for those who are in Christ Jesus," and we are in Him. God doesn't even remember our sins. He has erased them and forgotten them, too. What can be better that this? Begin today sharing Jesus and make a difference for Christ. This is our purpose now. Will you do it? If not, why not? I can help you if you need it.

18

HOW TO WITNESS IN THESE LAST DAYS

Let's begin with a strong statement from Jesus, "He who denies Me before man in this sinful and adulterous generation in no way will I acknowledge him before the Father and His holy angels." If this doesn't get your attention, stop reading, for this will be of no use to you.

When someone tells me their relationship with God is personal I know they aren't born again….yet! We must be bold and courteous in our evangelism. If you practice your smile before you go, doors will open automatically to hear what you have to say. I believe Jesus smiled all the time except when being attacked by the Pharisees. These men were pretenders and refused to recognize Him and the message Jesus was delivering from the Father. Let's decide now we will never be like them.

Unless we are willing to spend time with the Lord early in the morning before going out we won't be fresh. Jesus is the Light of the world and when you spend time with Him your face will shine as Moses did. Let's also remember Moses was not a good speaker but he was a man like David, a man after the heart of God.

If you are like David and Moses many will come to know Jesus by your testimony, for the Holy Spirit will make a way for it. John 3:16 is a great verse in the Word of God but it can not win souls alone. If you want to see what I mean, walk up to someone and quote it smiling. Then wait and see if the person there before you accepts Jesus as their Lord and Savior. I believe you will stand there a very long time. However if you say afterwards, "May I tell you what this verse did for me?" there is a better than 50% chance they will allow you to share. Then you must make your story short and sweet unless they ask for more.

Another very effective way to witness requires a bit more

courage. After a short greeting ask this question with your best smile, "Why do you love Jesus?" Make it in a soft child like way and you are apt to get an answer. Some may stumble around trying to come up with an answer that they think will please you. If you have spent time with Jesus His Spirit is upon you so don't panic if they can't respond or act hostile towards you. The following is why I would rather have someone reject me than try to please me.

One morning while driving to Destin from Alabama, God told me, "Provoke them to anger, provoke them to thoughtfulness and provoke them to exuberant praise." This means we can be bold, for we hold the keys to the Kingdom of God for the lost.

Our testimony with the Gospel defeats Satan and actually disarms him as a liar, thief, murderer, and accuser of the brethren. He is your opponent. We who have Jesus have His Spirit within us and He is greater than Satan who is in the world. Satan hates God and wants to do all he can to deprive Him of souls. Are you willing to let him have the souls where you live?

I'm not willing to give them up that easily and have witnessed for over 30 years to anyone standing still and to some who were walking away. Some have become martyrs doing this but after many hundreds of thousands I haven't even been spit upon. Perhaps one day witnessing may cost me my earthly life, but it sure can't cost me my eternal life nor can it yours. If you are born again your name is enrolled in the small Book of Life. If you are only a religious person you are already in real danger. If I were you, I would go to my knees now and ask the Holy Spirit to take me to the cross.

Then while looking up at Jesus, drink in the level of brutality He suffered for you. Let it continue to sink in until you love Him more than anyone you know. Now tell Him how you feel about your sinful past. He already knows it but admitting it will set you free.

Now ask Him to forgive you and His response will always be YES! Then humbly ask Him to come into your heart as your

Lord. Now inbreathe His Spirit by faith. As you do you become a brand new creature, no longer deserving death as a sinner but now a saint of God living in a mortal body. God has adopted you and you are now a member of His family, too. Ask the Lord to lead you to a pastor who can baptize you. He will also watch over you as you grow in Jesus. Glory Hallelujah! God is so Good!

If you want more help, write to me real soon for time is short now.

19

DESTINATION HEAVEN

In Matthew 25 we see Jesus calling the virgins waiting on Him one of two names, prudent and foolish. The difference was their relationship with Him. Those who had become born again [filled with His Spirit] were allowed into the Wedding Feast. Those who had refused, and were comfortable without a relationship, were called "foolish." Why in the world would anyone be so foolish? Simple, they loved the world and what it offered more than Him.

There will be anguish on the day God separates the sheep from the goats. The Bible tells us there will be weeping and wailing and gnashing of teeth.

This message is to help you to not be one of them in such

despair. If you are willing to accept what it's going to teach, you'll be as safe as the people and animals in Noah's ark. Do you remember the story of how God destroyed the earth with a flood? Please read the account in Genesis. There are several very important things to notice. First, the world had become very wicked [like it is now]. Two, God had a plan of redemption but it required a faithful man [Noah] to obey Him [like we must now]. Three, God closed the door to the ark before the rain began [Jesus closes the door to the foolish]. It won't be opened again either until the storm is over.

God has warned us that He will not strive with man forever. If you're refusing to surrender your life to Jesus, He'll bar the door to you. If you accept His Lordship, He will say, "Well done My good and faithful servant, enter now into the Joy of Your Master."

He calls us servants, for our hearts were changed at our new birth and became those who fed the hungry, gave drink to the thirsty, clothed the naked, and showed hospitality to the lost and homeless. We obeyed without being prodded, for the Spirit of Jesus was inside us. His Love was flowing like a spring of living water to those who would drink from it.

Are you willing? Tell Him, and you'll find more JOY than you can handle. But remember, it's only a taste of what's yours throughout eternity in Heaven.

ABOUT THE AUTHOR

Capt. Ben Marler is a layman, and yet he has been an evangelist for most of his life. Raised in the Episcopal Church, he accepted Jesus into his heart at a very young age. He was born again at age 31 and filled with the Holy Spirit on May 23, 1971. Under the influence of the Holy Spirit when he read a verse of scripture, which seemed to be enlarged and illuminated on its page, Ephesians 2:10 ("For we are His workmanship, created in Christ Jesus, for good works which He has prepared in advance for us to walk in") suddenly, his life was pointed in a very new direction.

He thought that he was being called into the ministry and should go to seminary. But that was not what God planned. Instead, God brought people to him and used him exactly where he was.

You see, his name was becoming synonymous with fishing

and Destin.

For 36 years, he had an audience of fishermen, customers, who came for miles to go fishing out of the sportsmen's paradise called Destin, Florida. He taught literally hundreds of thousands of people to fish in a famous fishing lesson based on the book of Genesis.

Capt. Ben has a strong and genuine love for people, along with a folksy way with words that seems to inspire others to know and serve Jesus. Since his retirement from the fishing business, he has dedicated his life to daily writings to encourage other Christians to live for Jesus, and to spread the Gospel, in every way they can.

"God will use you. You only have to ask him."

This is Captain Ben Marler's third book. He lives in Destin, Florida with his large "Tribe" of wife, daughters, sons in law, grandchildren and great grandchildren and extended family.

OTHER BOOKS BY CAPT. BEN MARLER

"Old Destin, Through the Eyes of a Child" (ISBN 10: 1461098556)

"4 o'clock in the morning In a Sleepy Fishing Village Called Destin-Living an Exciting Life Sharing Jesus according to Eph. 2:10" (ISBN 10: 1467952958)

Available at Amazon.com, CreatespaceDirect.com, and Other Fine Retailers.

http://olddestin.blogspot.com

http://4oclockinthemorningdestin.blogspot.com

Capt. Ben Marler, 3857 Indian Trail, Unit 502, Destin, FL 32541 E-mail: captben61@gmail.com

Capt. Ben Marler is on facebook as Ben Marler

And on twitter as captben61

OLD DESTIN
Through the eyes
of a Child

Capt. Ben Marler

4

o' clock

in the

mornin

In a Sleepy Fishing Village Called Destin

Living an Exciting Life Sharing Jesus according to Eph 2:10

The Author of Old Destin Through the Eyes of a Child
Capt. Ben Marler